80% OF

QUR'ANIC

WORDS

— ❋ —

Classified word lists
for easy memorisation

Compiled by
Dr Abdulazeez Abdulraheem

Islamic Book Trust
Kuala Lumpur

Reprint 2020

Published 2009 by
Islamic Book Trust
607 Mutiara Majestic
Jalan Othman
46000 Petaling Jaya
Selangor, Malaysia
www.ibtbooks.com

Islamic Book Trust is affiliated with The Other Press.

Issued with The Holy Qur'an, Text Translation and Commentary
by Abdullah Yusuf Ali and The Message of the Qur'an by
Muhammad Asad, a monumental work widely recognised, since
1934, as an authorative translation of the Holy Qur'an in
English with 6,310 notes, 11 appendices and a comprehensive
index. For details please visit www.ibtbooks.com

The compiler of this booklet can be reached at:
azeez1961@hotmail.com

List of abbreviations

mg	masculine gender
fg	feminine gender
br. pl	broken plural
sg	singular
dl	dual
pl	plural
sb	somebody
st	something
ss	somebody or something

Preface

All praise be to Allah, and may peace and blessings of Allah be upon His Prophet, Muhammad. Allah says very explicitly in His Book;

> *(Here is) a Book which We have sent down unto you, full of blessings that they may ponder over its signs, and that men of understanding may receive admonition."* [38:29]

If we don't understand the Book, how can we ponder on its verses! The Prophet of Allah, Muhammad (ṣ). said,

> The best among you are those who have learnt the Qur'an and teach it (to others)" [*Ṣaḥīḥ Bukhārī*].

This booklet is prepared to give at least some help in fulfilling the abovementioned objectives. Please keep the following points in mind (in addition to those listed on the back cover) while studying this booklet:

1. When there are more than one distinctly different meanings of a word, a semicolon is placed between

the two meanings. For similar meanings, a comma is placed between the meanings. For example: (eye; spring عَيْن) and (above, up عَلَى).

2. If the last letter of a word given in this booklet does not have a vowel sign ( ), it indicates that any vowel sign can come on it depending upon the context in which that word is used. If الْ occurs before the word, then Tanwīn ( ) is not used.

3. At the bottom left of the page, total is provided for the number of times the words of that page have occurred in the Qur'an. The bottom right shows the percent of the total Qur'anic words that you have learnt so far, if you have memorized the meanings the words till that page.

4. In almost every case, the words are arranged alphabetically to make the search easy.

5. The word forms related to dual number and feminine gender are used sparingly in the Holy Qur'an. Therefore, these forms may be given less emphasis in the beginning stages.

6. For almost every verb type, samples of the معروف forms (active voice) are provided in the first line

those of the مجهول forms (passive voice) in the last.

7.   Just like in any language, some verbs and nouns of action are always followed by a preposition. For example, believe in: آمَنَ بِ.

However, in some cases, a change in preposition may change the meanings too, for example, get; get in; get at; get by, get off, get on, etc. A list of some important verbs along with changing prepositions is provided on page no. 34.

Abdul Azeez Abdulraheem

Acknowledgements

Many people have contributed in the compilation of this booklet. I have received significant help on different aspects of this work from my wife, Tabinda Tahseen, and from my colleagues, Dr M.A. Mohiuddin, Mr M. Na'eemuddin, and Mr M. Abdul Bari. May Allah reward them all.

Important References:
قائمة معجمية بألفاظ القرآن الكريم ودرجات تكرارها:
د. محمد حسين أبو الفتوح. مكتبة لبنان. لبنان 1990.
المعجم المفهرس لألفاظ القرآن الكريم: محمد فؤاد عبد الباقي.

This, that...!

this	(mg)	هَٰذَا
that	(mg)	ذَٰلِكَ
this	(fg)	هَٰذِه
that	(fg)	تِلْكَ
these	(mg/fg)	هَٰؤُلَاء
those	(mg/fg)	أُولَٰئِكَ
he who	(mg)	الَّذِي
she who	(fg)	الَّتِي
those who	(mg)	الَّذِينَ
these	(for br. pl)	هَٰذِه
those	(for br. pl)	تِلْكَ
those who	(for br. pl)	الَّتِي

No, No!!!

(There is) no god		لَا إِلَٰهَ
except Allah		إِلَّا الله
never, certainly not		كَلَّا
not	(for future)	لَنْ
not	(for past)	لَمْ
not		مَا
not	(fg)	لَيْسَ (لَيْسَت)
yes, indeed		بَلَى
not, other than		غَيْر
besides; less than		دُونَ
except; unless; if not		إِلَّا
yes		نَعَمْ

Whose?			Who?	
his	(mg)	...ه	he (mg)	هُوَ
their	(mg)	...هُمْ	them (mg)	هُمْ
your	(mg)	...كَ	you (mg)	أَنْتَ
your	(mg)	...كُمْ	you all (mg)	أَنْتُم
my	(me)	...ي (ني)	i (mg/fg)	أَنَا
us	(mg/fg)	...نَا	we (mg/fg)	نَحْنُ
her	(fg)	...هَا	she (fg)	هِيَ
their	(fg)	...هُنَّ	they (fg)	هُنَّ
your	(fg)	...كِ	you (fg)	أَنْتِ
their	(for br. pl)	...هَا	they (for br. pl)	هِيَ
their	(dl)	...هُمَا	those two (dl)	هُمَا
your (dl)		...كُمَا	you two (dl)	أَنْتُمَا

Where?   # Questions!?

above, up	فَوْق	what?, that which	مَا
under	تَحْت	who?, the one who	مَنْ
in front of	بَيْنَ أَيْدِي، بَيْنَ يَدَيْ	when?, the time when	مَتَى
back, after	خَلْف	where?	أَيْنَ
in front of	أَمَام	how?	كَيْفَ
behind	وَرَاء	how many?	كَمْ
right; oath	يَمِين (أَيْمَان pl)	which?	أَيُّ
left	شِمَال (شَمَائِل pl)	where from?, why?	أَنَّى
between	بَيْن	Is? Am? Are? Do? Have?	أَ، هَل
around	حَوْل	what?	مَاذَا
wherever	حَيْثُ	why?	لِمَ، لِمَاذَا
wherever	أَيْنَمَا	if not; why not	لَوْ لَا

Words (from first 6 pages): 32263   [3]   Percent (first 6 pages): 41.5

# Miscellaneous		# When?	
endowed with; owner of	*(mg)* ذُو، ذَا، ذِي	before	قَبْلَ
endowed with; owner of	*(fg)* ذَات	after	بَعْد
people of; owners of	أُوْلُوا، أُوْلِي	time, period; at the time of	حِين
people of; relative	أَهْل	when *(for past)*	إِذْ
family, relatives, people	آل	when *(for future)*	إِذَا
lo!; do not?, will not?	أَلَا	then	ثُمَّ
what an excellent...	نِعْمَ	then, thus, therefore	فَ
what an evil...	بِئْسَ	nay, -- rather, but, however	بَل
evil is that which	بِئْسَمَا	near, with	عِنْدَ، لَدَى، لَدُنْ
something similar	مِثْل	nothing --- but	إِنْ ... إِلَّا
similitude	مَثَل (أَمْثَال)	nothing --- but	مَا ... إِلَّا
than the one who; from those who	مِمَّن (مِنْ+مَنْ)	that...not; so as not to	أَلَّا (أَنْ+لَا)

Prepositions + مَا		Prepositions	
with what, because	بِمَا	with, in, from,…	بِ
about what	عَمَّا	about	عَنْ
in what	فِيمَا	in	فِي
as, just as	كَمَا	as, like	كَ
for what; for that which	لِمَا	for	لِ، لَ
out of what	مِمَّا	from	مِنْ
as to, as for	أَمَّا	towards	إِلَى
if; either/or	إِمَّا	by (of oath)	تَ
that	أَنَّمَا	until	حَتَّى
verily; is but	إِنَّمَا	on	عَلَى
as if	كَأَنَّمَا	with	مَعَ
whenever	كُلَّمَا	and; by (of oath)	وَ

Prefix for verb,...		Inna	
has (with مَاضِي) ; surely (with مُضارع)	قَدْ (+فعل)	verily, truly	إِنَّ
will (for near future)	سَ (+فعل)	that	أَنَّ
will (for future)	سَوْفَ (+فعل)	as if	كَأَنَّ
will surely	لَ+فعل+نَّ	but, however	لَكِنَّ (لكِنْ)
indeed	لَقَدْ (+فعل)	perhaps, may be	لَعَلَّ
indeed, surely	لَ	that	أَنْ
let sb do (imperative)	لِ، لْ (أَمْر)	if	إِنْ
the	الْ	alone	إِيَّا
or?	أَمْ	possibly	عَسَى
or	أَوْ	when	لَمَّا
some of	بَعْض	if	لَوْ
everyone; all	كُلُّ	O!	يَا، يَاأَيُّهَا

Words (from first 6 pages): 32263   [6]   Percent (first 6 pages): 41.5

Some attributes (of Allah and others)

knowing, ever aware	خَبِير	45	first	أَوَّل (أُولَى) (fg)	82
Lord; Sustainer	رَبّ	970	last	آخِر (آخِرَة) (fg)	40
Compassionate	رَحْمَٰن	57	[other]	آخَر (أُخْرَى) (fg)	65
peace	سَلَام	42	trustworthy	أَمِين	14
one who listens	سَمِيع	47	one who sees clearly	بَصِير	53
grateful	شَكُور	24	far	بَعِيد	25
mighty	عَزِيز	99	most forgiving	تَوَّاب	11
most forgiving	غَفُور	91	protector	حَفِيظ	26
All-powerful	قَدِير	45	wise	حَكِيم	97
warner	نَذِير	44	forbearing	حَلِيم	15
strong helper	نَصِير	24	praiseworthy	حَمِيد	17
one who takes care of a thing for another	وَكِيل	24	warm (friend); boiling water	حَمِيم	20

Noun of Superiority اسم تَفْضِيل			Some attributes...		
most severe	أَشَدّ	31	severe; strong	شَدِيد	52
higher, superior	أَعْلَى	11	high, exalted	عَلِيّ	11
better-knowing, more informed	أَعْلَم	49	knower	عَلِيم	162
nearer	أَقْرَب	19	near	قَرِيب	26
bigger	أَكْبَر	23	big	كَبِير (كَبِيرَة fg)	44
more; most	أَكْثَر	80	plenty; much	كَثِير (كَثِيرَة fg)	74
better	أَحْسَن	36	quick; swift; fast	سَرِيع	10
more entitled; more worthy	أَحَقّ	10	merciful	رَحِيم	182
nearer; more likely; lower; less	أَدْنَى	12	supreme	عَظِيم	107
more unjust	أَظْلَم	16	little	قَلِيل (قَلِيلَة fg)	71
better guided	أَهْدَى	7	noble; honourable; generous	كَرِيم	27
nearer, closer; woe	أَوْلَى	11	subtle	لَطِيف	7

Total words (of this pages): 1078   [8]   Percent so far: 45.4

Prophets and Allah's Signs

Messenger	رَسُول (رُسُل *pl*)	332	sign	آيَة (آيَات *pl*)	382
Prophet	نَبِيّ	75	evidence	بَيِّنَة (بَيِّنَات *pl*)	71
Prophets	نَبِيُّون، نَبِيِّين، أَنْبِيَاء		Qur'an; reading, recitation	قُرْآن	70
	آدَم، نُوح، إِبْرَاهِيم،	137	cattle	أَنْعَام	32
	لُوط، إِسْمَاعِيل، إِسْحَاق،	56	mountain	جَبَل (جِبَال *pl*)	39
	يَعْقُوب (إِسْرَائيل) يُوسُف،	86	sea; large river	بَحْر	38
	هُود، شُعَيْب، صَالِح،	30	sun	شَمْس	33
	مُوسَى، عِيسَى ابْن مَرْيَم	195	moon	قَمَر	33
Satan	شَيْطَان (شَيَاطِين *pl*)	88	night	لَيْل	80
Pharaoh	فِرْعَوْن	74	day	نَهَار	57
People of Hud	عَاد	24	earth	أَرْض	461
People of Salih	ثَمُود	26	sky	سَمَاء (سَمَاوَات *pl*)	310

Total words (of this pages): 2729   [9]   Percent so far: 48.9

Last day

companion, fellow	صَاحِب (أَصْحَاب)	94	forever; ever	أَبَداً	28
end	عَاقِبَة	32	reward	أَجْر (أُجُور *pl*)	105
torment	عَذَاب	332	term	أَجَل	52
chastisement (as a result of sin)	عِقَاب	20	the Hereafter	الْآخِرَة	115
Resurrection	قِيَامَة	70	painful	أَلِيم	72
meeting	لِقَاء	24	reward	ثَوَاب	13
fixed	مُسَمَّى	21	hellfire	جَحِيم	26
fire	نَار	145	reward	جَزَاء	42
river	نَهَر (أَنْهَار *pl*)	54	garden	جَنَّة (جَنَّات *pl*)	147
woe unto ...	وَيْل	40	the hell	جَهَنَّم	77
day	يَوْم (أَيَّام *pl*)	393	reckoning	حِسَاب	39
that day	يَوْمَئِذٍ	70	hour (day of resurrection)	سَاعَة	47

Total words (of this pages): 2048   [10]   Percent so far: 51.6

Dīn

Faith

matter; affair	أَمْر (أُمُور pl)	13	one	أَحَد (إِحْدَى fg)	85
piety; fear; protection	تَقْوَى	17	god; deity	إِلَه (آلِهَة pl)	34
truth, true; right	حَقّ	247	partner, associate	شَرِيك (شُرَكَاء pl)	40
[falsehood	إبَاطِل	26	witness	شَهَادَة	26
wisdom	حِكْمَة	20	throne	عَرْش	26
praise	حَمْد	43	covenant, promise	عَهْد	29
religion; law; judgement	دِيْن	92	unseen	غَيْب	49
poor-due, charity	زَكَاة	32	book	كِتَاب (كُتُب pl)	261
witness, present	شَهِيد (شُهَدَاء pl)	56	word	كَلِمَة	42
prayer	صَلَاة	83	angel	مَلَك (مَلَائِكَة pl)	88
clear, self-expressive	مُبِين	119	covenant, treaty	مِيثَاق	25
light	نُور	43	one	وَاحِد (وَاحِدَة fg)	61

Total words (of this pages): 1557   [11]   Percent so far: 53.6

Deeds

actions, deeds, works	أَعْمَال *pl*	41
good (deed)	حَسَنَة (حَسَنَات *pl*)	31
evil, bad	سَيِّئَة (سَيِّئَات *pl*)	68
good, better	خَيْر	186
evil, bad, worse	شَرّ	29
sin	إِثْم	35
sin	ذَنْب (ذُنُوب *pl*)	37
sin	جُنَاح	25
unlawful	حَرَام	26
name	اسْم (أَسْمَاء *pl*)	27
discourse; speech	حَدِيث (أَحَادِيث *pl*)	23
good	طَيِّبَة (طَيِّبَات *pl*)	30

Blessings

favours	آلَاء	34
authority; warrant	سُلْطَان	37
grace	فَضْل	84
water	مَاء	63
dominion, reign	مُلْك	48
favour	نِعْمَة	37
all	أَجْمَعُون، أَجْمَعِين	26
permission	إِذْن	39
punishment; power; adversity	بَأْس	25
all, everybody	جَمِيع	53
same; equals; level; fair	سَوَاء	27
party, group	فَرِيق	33

Total words (of this pages): 1064   [12]   Percent so far: 53.6

Relatives

mother	أُمّ (أُمَّهَات pl)	35
father	أَب، أَبَت (آبَاء pl)	117
wife; husband	زَوْج (أَزْوَاج pl)	76
man	رَجُل (رِجَال pl)	57
woman	امْرَأَة (نِسَاء pl)	83
child	وَلَد (أَوْلَاد pl)	56
father	وَالِد (وَالِدَيْن dl)	20
descendants; children	ذُرِّيَّة	32
son	ابْن	41
sons	بَنُون، بَنِين، أَبْنَاء pl	22
brother	أَخ (أَخُو، أَخَا، أَخِي)	67
brothers	إِخْوَان pl	22

Self (body parts)

face	وَجْه (وُجُوه pl)	72
eye; spring	عَيْن (أَعْيُن pl)	47
sights	أَبْصَار pl	38
mouths	أَفْوَاه pl	21
tongue; language	لِسَان (أَلْسِنَة pl)	25
heart	قَلْب (قُلُوب pl)	132
breast	صَدْر (صُدُور pl)	44
hand	يَد (أَيْدِي pl)	118
foot	رِجْلٌ (أَرْجُل pl)	15
soul	نَفْس (أَنْفُس pl)	293
soul, spirit	رُوح	21
power, strength	قُوَّة	28

Total words (of this pages): 1482   [13]   Percent so far: 56.8

World

house	بَيْت (بُيُوت *pl*)	64
abode	دَار (دِيَار *pl*)	48
world	دُنْيَا	115
way	سَبِيل (سُبُل *pl*)	176
path	صِرَاط	46
world	عَالَم (عَالَمِين *pl*)	73
trial; persecution	فِتْنَة	34
town	قَرْيَة (قُرَى *pl*)	57
wealth	مَال (أَمْوَال *pl*)	86
provision; enjoyment	مَتَاع	34
mosque	مَسْجِد (مَسَاجِد *pl*)	28
place; abode	مَكَان (مَكَانَة)	32

People

community	أُمَّة (أُمَم *pl*)	64
people	قَوْم	383
man	إِنْسَان	65
men, people	نَاس	248
male	ذَكَر (ذُكُور *pl*)	16
female	أُنْثَى (إِنَاث *pl*)	30
slave	عَبْد (عِبَاد *pl*)	126
enemy	عَدُوّ (أَعْدَاء *pl*)	44
disbelievers	كُفَّار	21
criminal	مُجْرِم	52
chiefs, leaders	مَلَأ	22
protecting friend; guardian	وَلِيّ (أَوْلِيَاء *pl*)	86

Total words (of this pages): 1950   [14]   Percent so far: 59.3

فِعْل ثلاثي مُجَرَّد فَتَحَ يَفْتَحُ

to do	فِعْل	فَاعِل	اِفْعَلْ	يَفْعَلُ	فَعَلَ	105
to open, to give victory	فَتْح	فَاتِح	اِفْتَحْ	يَفْتَحُ	فَتَحَ	29
to raise; to resurrect	بَعْث	بَاعِث	اِبْعَثْ	يَبْعَثُ	بَعَثَ	65
to make, to place, to set up	جَعْل	جَاعِل	اِجْعَلْ	يَجْعَلُ	جَعَلَ	346
to gather, to collect	جَمْع	جَامِع	اِجْمَعْ	يَجْمَعُ	جَمَعَ	40
to go	ذِهَاب	ذَاهِب	اِذْهَبْ	يَذْهَبُ	ذَهَبَ	35
to raise	رَفْع	رَافِع	اِرْفَعْ	يَرْفَعُ	رَفَعَ	28
to enchant, to bewitch	سِحْر	سَاحِر	اِسْحَرْ	يَسْحَرُ	سَحَرَ	49
to act righteously	مَصْلَحَة	صَالِح	اِصْلَحْ	يَصْلَحُ	صَلَحَ	131
to curse	لَعْن	لَاعِن	اِلْعَنْ	يَلْعَنُ	لَعَنَ	27
to profit	نَفْع	نَافِع	اِنْفَعْ	يَنْفَعُ	نَفَعَ	42
passive voice مَجْهُول ←		مَفْعُول		يُفْعَلُ	فُعِلَ	

فِعل ثُلاثِي مُجَرَّد نَصَرَ يَنْصُرُ

	فِعل	فَاعِل	أُفْعُل	يَفْعُلُ	فَعَلَ	
to help; to deliver	نَصْر	نَاصِر	أُنْصُرْ	يَنْصُرُ	نَصَرَ	92
to reach	بُلُوغ	بَالِغ	أُبْلُغْ	يَبْلُغُ	بَلَغَ	49
to leave	تَرْك	تَارِك	أُتْرُكْ	يَتْرُكُ	تَرَكَ	43
to gather; to bring together	حَشْر	حَاشِر	أُحْشُرْ	يَحْشُرُ	حَشَرَ	43
to judge; to rule	حُكْم	حَاكِم	أُحْكُمْ	يَحْكُمُ	حَكَمَ	80
to come out	خُرُوج	خَارِج	أُخْرُجْ	يَخْرُجُ	خَرَجَ	61
to live forever	خُلُود	خَالِد	أُخْلُدْ	يَخْلُدُ	خَلَدَ	83
to create out of nothing	خَلْق	خَالِق	أُخْلُقْ	يَخْلُقُ	خَلَقَ	248
to enter	دُخُول	دَاخِل	أُدْخُلْ	يَدْخُلُ	دَخَلَ	78
to remember	ذِكْر	ذَاكِر	اذْكُرْ	يَذْكُرُ	ذَكَرَ	163
to provide	رِزْق	رَازِق	أُرْزُقْ	يَرْزُقُ	رَزَقَ	122

Total words (of this pages): 1062   [16]   Percent so far: 61.86

فِعل ثُلاثِي مُجَرَّد نَصَر يَنصُرُ

to prostrate	سُجُود	ساجِد	اُسْجُدْ	يَسْجُدُ	سَجَدَ	49
to perceive	شُعُور	شاعِر	اُشْعُرْ	يَشْعُرُ	شَعَرَ	29
to be grateful	شُكْر	شاكِر	اُشْكُرْ	يَشْكُرُ	شَكَرَ	63
to be true; to say the truth	صِدْق	صادِق	اُصْدُقْ	يَصْدُقُ	صَدَقَ	89
to worship; to serve	عِبادَة	عابِد	اُعْبُدْ	يَعْبُدُ	عَبَدَ	143
to transgress	فِسْق	فاسِق	اُفْسُقْ	يَفْسُقُ	فَسَقَ	54
to kill; to slay	قَتْل	قاتِل	اُقْتُلْ	يَقْتُلُ	قَتَلَ	93
to sit; to remain behind	قُعُود	قاعِد	اُقْعُدْ	يَقْعُدُ	قَعَدَ	23
to prescribe; to write	كِتابَة	كاتِب	اُكْتُبْ	يَكْتُبُ	كَتَبَ	56
to disbelieve; to be ungrateful	كُفْر	كافِر	اُكْفُرْ	يَكْفُرُ	كَفَرَ	461
to plot	مَكْر	ماكِر	اُمْكُرْ	يَمْكُرُ	مَكَرَ	43
to look; to wait	نَظَر	ناظِر	اُنْظُرْ	يَنْظُرُ	نَظَرَ	95

Total words (of this pages): 1198   [17]   Percent so far: 63.4

فِعْل ثُلَاثِي مُجَرَّد ضَرَبَ يَضرِبُ

	فِعْل	فَاعِل	افْعِل	يَفْعِلُ	فَعَلَ	
to strike	ضَرْب	ضَارِب	اضْرِب	يَضرِبُ	ضَرَبَ	58
to carry; to bear	حَمْل	حَامِل	احْمِل	يَحْمِلُ	حَمَلَ	50
to bear with patience	صَبْر	صَابِر	اصْبِر	يَصبِرُ	صَبَرَ	94
to wrong	ظُلْم	ظَالِم	اظْلِمْ	يَظْلِمُ	ظَلَمَ	266
to recognise	مَعْرِفَة	عَارِف	اعْرِف	يَعْرِفُ	عَرَفَ	59
to understand; to comprehend	عَقْل	عَاقِل	اعْقِل	يَعْقِلُ	عَقَلَ	49
to forgive; to cover	مَغْفِرَة	غَافِر	اغْفِر	يَغْفِرُ	غَفَرَ	95
to decree; to have power;	قَدْر، قُدْرَة	قَادِر	اقْدِر	يَقْدِرُ	قَدَرَ	47
to lie	كَذِب	كَاذِب	اكْذِب	يَكْذِبُ	كَذَبَ	76
to earn	كَسْب	كَاسِب	اكْسِب	يَكْسِبُ	كَسَبَ	62
to possess	مِلْك	مَالِك	امْلِك	يَمْلِكُ	مَلَكَ	49

Total words (of this pages): 905   [18]   Percent so far: 64.6

فِعل ثُلَاثِي مُجَرَّد سَمِعَ يَسْمَعُ

	فِعْل	فَاعِل	اِفْعَلْ	يَفْعَلُ	فَعِلَ	
to hear	سَمَاعَة	سَامِع	اِسْمَعْ	يَسْمَعُ	سَمِعَ	100
to be grieved	حُزْن	حَازِن	اِحْزَنْ	يَحْزَنُ	حَزِنَ	30
to think; to consider	حَسْب	حَاسِب	اِحْسَبْ	يَحْسَبُ	حَسِبَ	46
to guard; to protect	حِفْظ	حَافِظ	اِحْفَظْ	يَحْفَظُ	حَفِظَ	27
to lose	خُسْر	خَاسِر	اِخْسَرْ	يَخْسَرُ	خَسِرَ	51
to have mercy on someone	رَحْمَة	رَاحِم	اِرْحَمْ	يَرْحَمُ	رَحِمَ	148
to bear witness; to be present	شُهُود	شَاهِد	اِشْهَدْ	يَشْهَدُ	شَهِدَ	66
to know	عِلْم	عَالِم	اِعْلَمْ	يَعْلَمُ	عَلِمَ	518
to work; to do	عَمَل	عَامِل	اِعْمَلْ	يَعْمَلُ	عَمِلَ	318
to dislike; to detest	كُرْه	كَارِه	اِكْرَهْ	يَكْرَهُ	كَرِهَ	25
to watch; to see	بَصَر	بَاصِر	اُبْصُرْ	يَبْصُرُ	بَصِرَ	13

Total words (of this pages): 1342　　[19]　　Percent so far: 66.29

The last two letters of the root are same   فِعْل ثُلَاثِي مُجَرَّد مُضَاعَف

	(فُلَّ، يُفَلُّ)	فَلَّ ...	افلِل، أُفْلُل فَالَ	يَفَلُّ، يَفِلُّ	فَلَّ	
to live; to greet	حَيَاة	حَيَّ	احْيَ	يَحْيَا	حَيَّ	83
to give back; to return	رَدّ	رَادّ	أُرْدُدْ	يَرُدُّ	رَدَّ	45
to turn away; to hinder	صَدّ	صَادّ	أُصْدُدْ	يَصُدُّ	صَدَّ	39
to hurt; to harm	ضَرّ	ضَارّ	أُضْرُرْ	يَضُرُّ	ضَرَّ	31
to go astray; to err; to waste	ضَلَالَة	ضَالّ	اضْلِلْ	يَضِلُّ	ضَلَّ	113
to think; to believe	ظَنّ	ظَانّ	أُظْنُنْ	يَظُنُّ	ظَنَّ	68
to count	عَدّ	عَادّ	أُعْدُدْ	يَعُدُّ	عَدَّ	17
to beguile	غُرُور	غَارّ	اغْرُرْ	يَغُرُّ	غَرَّ	24
to spread out; to stretch	مَدّ	مَادّ	أُمْدُدْ	يَمُدُّ	سَدَّ	17
to touch	مَسّ	مَاسّ	امْسِسْ	يَمَسُّ	مَسَّ	58
to love; to wish	وُدّ	وَادّ	أَوْدَدْ	يَوَدُّ	وَدَّ	18

Total words (of this pages): 513   [20]   Percent so far: 67

First letter of the root is و or ي				فِعل ثُلَاثي مُجَرَّد مِثَال	
(وُعِلَ، يُوعَلُ)	وَعْل	وَاعِل	عَلْ، يَعلُ، عِلْ	يَعَلُ، يَعِلُ	وَعَلَ
to leave behind	وَذْر	وَاذِر	ذَرْ	يَذَرُ	وَذَرَ 45
to put; to set	وُضْع	وَاضِع	ضَعْ	يَضَعُ	وَضَعَ 22
to befall	وَقُوع	وَاقِع	قَعْ	يَقَعُ	وَقَعَ 20
to grant	وَهْب	وَاهِب	هَبْ	يَهَبُ	وَهَبَ 23
to find	وُجُود	وَاجِد	جِدْ	يَجِدُ	وَجَدَ 107
to inherit	وَرَاثَة	وَارِث	رِثْ	يَرِثُ	وَرِثَ 19
to bear a load	وِزْر	وَازِر	زِرْ	يَزِرُ	وَزَرَ 19
to describe; to ascribe	وَصْف	وَاصِف	صِفْ	يَصِفُ	وَصَفَ 14
to promise	وَعْد	وَاعِد	عِدْ	يَعِدُ	وَعَدَ 124
to protect; to save	وِقَايَة	وَاقٍ	قِ	يَقِي	وَقَى 19
to embrace; to comprehend	سَعَة	وَاسِع	اِيسَعْ	يَوَسَعُ	وَسِعَ 25

	(فِيلَ، يُفَالُ) فَوْل..	فَائِل	فُلْ،.. يُفَوْلُ،..	فَالَ	
to repent	تَوْبَة	تَائِب	تُبْ	يَتُوبُ	تَابَ 72
to taste	ذَوْق	ذَائِق	ذُقْ	يَذُوقُ	ذَاقَ 42
to succeed; to gain victory	فَوْز	فَائِز	فُزْ	يَفُوزُ	فَازَ 26
to say	قَوْل	قَائِل	قُلْ	يَقُولُ	قَالَ 1719
to stand up; to raise	قِيام	قَائِم	قُمْ	يَقُومُ	قَامَ 55
to be	كَوْن	كَائِن	كُنْ	يَكُونُ	كَانَ 1361
to die	مَوْت	مَائِت	مُتْ	يَمُوتُ	مَاتَ 93
to be afraid	خَوْف	خَائِف	خفْ	يَخَافُ	خَافَ 112
to become nigh; to be close to	كَوْد	كَائِد	كِدْ	يَكَادُ	كَادَ 24
to plot against	كَيْد	كَائِد	كِدْ	يَكِيدُ	كَادَ 35
to increase	زِيَادَة	زَائِد	زِدْ	يَزِيدُ	زَادَ 51

فِعل ثُلَاثِي مُجَرَّد أَجْوَف — Second letter of the root is و or ي

Total words (of this pages): 3590   [22]   Percent so far: 72.13

Last letter of the root is و or ي				فِعل ثُلَاثِي مُجَرَّد نَاقِص		
to recite	تِلَاوَة	تَالٍ	اُتْلُ	يَتْلُو	تَلَا	61
to call; to pray	دُعَاء	دَاعٍ	اُدْعُ	يَدْعُو	دَعَا	197
to forgo	عَفْو	عَافٍ	أعفُ	يَعفُو	عَفَا	30
to want, to seek	بَغْى	بَاغٍ	اِبْغِ	يَبْغِي	بَغَى	29
to flow	جَرَيَان	جَارٍ	اِجْرِ	يَجْرِي	جَرَى	60
to reward	جَزَاء	جَازٍ	اِجْزِ	يَجْزِي	جَزَى	116
to decree; to fulfil	قَضَاء	قَاضٍ	اِقْضِ	يَقْضِي	قَضَى	62
to suffice	كِفَايَة	كَافٍ	اِكْفِ	يَكْفِي	كَفَى	32
to guide; to direct	هُدْى	هَادٍ	اِهْدِ	يَهْدِي	هَدَى	163
to fear	خَشِيَّة	خَاشٍ	اِخْشَ	يَخْشَى	خَشِيَ	48
to be satisfied, to be content	رِضْوَان	رَاضٍ	اِرْضَ	يَرْضَى	رَضِيَ	57
to forget	نِسْيَان	نَاسٍ	اِنْسَ	يَنْسَى	نَسِيَ	36

Anyone of the 3 letters of the root is hamzah   فِعل ثُلَاثِي مَهْمُوز

to ask	سُؤَال	سَائِل	سَلْ	يَسْأَلُ	سَأَلَ	119
to read; to recite	قِرَاءَة	قَارِئ	اقْرَأْ	يَقْرَأُ	قَرَأَ	17
to take; to catch	أَخْذ	آخِذ	خُذْ	يَأْخُذُ	أَخَذَ	142
to eat	أَكْل	آكِل	كُلْ	يَأْكُلُ	أَكَلَ	101
to command	أَمْر	آمِر	مُرْ	يَأْمُرُ	أَمَرَ	232
to be safe; to feel safe; to trust	أَمْن	آمِن	ائْمَنْ	يَأْمَنُ	أَمِنَ	25
to refuse	إِبَاء	آبٍ	ائْب	يَأْبَى	أَبَى	13
to see	رَأْي	رَاءٍ	رَ	يَرَى	رَأَى	269
to come	اِتْيَان	آتٍ	ائْت	يَأْتِي	أَتَى	263
to will, to wish	مَشِيئَة	شَاءٍ	شَأْ	يَشَاءُ	شَاءَ	277
to be evil	سَوْء	سَاوِئ	سُؤْ	يَسُوءُ	سَاءَ	39
to come	مَجِيء	جَاءٍ	جِئْ	يَجِيءُ	جَاءَ	236

Total words (of this pages): 1733   [24]   Percent so far: 75.51

Extra on (ˊ) 2nd letter of فَعَلَ (Third person, sing., masc.)			فِعل ثُلاثِي مَزِيد فِيه فَعَّل		
تَفْعِيل	مُفَعِّل	فَعِّل	يُفَعِّل	فَعَّل	
to change	تَبْدِيل	مُبَدِّل	بَدِّلْ	يُبَدِّلُ	بَدَّلَ	33
to give good news	تَبْشِير	مُبَشِّر	بَشِّرْ	يُبَشِّرُ	بَشَّرَ	48
to make clear	تَبْيِين	مُبَيِّن	بَيِّنْ	يُبَيِّنُ	بَيَّنَ	35
to adorn/make st to seem fair	تَزْيِين	مُزَيِّن	زَيِّنْ	يُزَيِّنُ	زَيَّنَ	26
to glorify; to praise	تَسْبِيح	مُسَبِّح	سَبِّحْ	يُسَبِّحُ	سَبَّحَ	48
to bring under control	تَسْخِير	مُسَخِّر	سَخِّرْ	يُسَخِّرُ	سَخَّرَ	26
to pronounce ss to be true	تَصْدِيق	مُصَدِّق	صَدِّقْ	يُصَدِّقُ	صَدَّقَ	31
to punish; to torment	تَعْذِيب	مُعَذِّب	عَذِّبْ	يُعَذِّبُ	عَذَّبَ	49
to teach	تَعْلِيم	مُعَلِّم	عَلِّمْ	يُعَلِّمُ	عَلَّمَ	42
to send forward	تَقْدِيم	مُقَدِّم	قَدِّمْ	يُقَدِّمُ	قَدَّمَ	27
to accuse ss of falsehood	تَكْذِيب	مُكَذِّب	كَذِّبْ	يُكَذِّبُ	كَذَّبَ	198

Total words (of this pages): 563   [25]   Percent so far: 76.2

	فِعل ثُلَاثِي مَزِيد فِيه فَعَّلَ، فَاعَلَ				Extra on (ّ) 2nd letter of فَعَلَ Extra alif in فَعَلَ	
46	نَبَّأَ	يُنَبِّئُ	نَبِّئْ	مُنَبِّئ	تَنْبِئَة	to declare; to apprise
79	نَزَّلَ	يُنَزِّلُ	نَزِّلْ	مُنَزِّل	تَنْزِيل	to send down
39	نَجَّى	يُنَجِّي	نَجِّ	مُنَجِّي	تَنْجِيَة	to deliver; to rescue
45	وَلَّى	يُوَلِّي	وَلِّ	مُوَلِّي	تَوْلِيَة	to turn
	فُعِّلَ	يُفَعَّلُ		مُفَعَّل	←	passive voice مجهول
	فَاعَلَ	يُفَاعِلُ	فَاعِلْ	مُفَاعِل	مُفَاعَلَة	
31	جَاهَدَ	يُجَاهِدُ	جَاهِدْ	مُجَاهِد	مُجَاهَدَة	to struggle; to strive
54	قَاتَلَ	يُقَاتِلُ	قَاتِلْ	مُقَاتِل	مُقَاتَلَة	to fight
44	نَادَى	يُنَادِي	نَادِ	مُنَادٍ	مُنَادَاة، نِدَاء	to call out; to cry unto
34	نَافَقَ	يُنَافِقُ	نَافِقْ	مُنَافِق	مُنَافَقَة	to play hypocrisy
24	هَاجَرَ	يُهَاجِرُ	هَاجِرْ	مُهَاجِر	مُهَاجَرَة	to migrate
	فُوعِلَ	يُفَاعِلُ		مُفَاعَل	←	passive voice مجهول

Extra on (ٔ) 2nd letter of نَعَلَ (Third person, sing., masc.)					فِعل ثُلاثِي مَزِيد فِيه أَفْعَلَ
	إِفْعال	مُفْعَل	أَفْعَلْ	يُفْعِلُ	أَفْعَلَ
to see; to watch	إِبْصار	مُبْصِر	أَبْصِرْ	يُبْصِرُ	أَبْصَرَ	36
to do good; to do excellently	إِحْسان	مُحْسِن	أَحْسِنْ	يُحْسِنُ	أَحْسَنَ	72
to bring forth	إِخْراج	مُخْرِج	أَخْرِجْ	يُخْرِجُ	أَخْرَجَ	108
to make ss enter	إِدْخال	مُدْخِل	أَدْخِلْ	يُدْخِلُ	أَدْخَلَ	45
to send back; to take back	إِرْجاع	مُرْجِع	أَرْجِعْ	يُرْجِعُ	أَرْجَعَ	33
to send	إِرْسال	مُرْسِل	أَرْسِلْ	يُرْسِلُ	أَرْسَلَ	135
to exceed; to be extravagant	إِسْراف	مُسْرِف	أَسْرِفْ	يُسْرِفُ	أَسْرَفَ	23
to submit; to surrender	إِسْلام	مُسْلِم	أَسْلَمْ	يُسْلِمُ	أَسْلَمَ	72
to ascribe a partner	إِشْراك	مُشْرِك	أَشْرِكْ	يُشْرِكُ	أَشْرَكَ	120
to become	إِصْباح	مُصْبِح	أَصْبَحْ	يُصْبِحُ	أَصْبَحَ	34
to become good; to make good	إِصْلاح	مُصْلِح	أَصْلِحْ	يُصْلِحُ	أَصْلَحَ	40

Total words (of this pages): 718   [27]   Percent so far: 77.7

Extra Hamzah before فَعَلَ (Third person, sing., masc.)					فِعل ثُلاثي مَزيد فيه أفعَلَ	
to turn away; to backslide	إعْراض	مُعْرِض	أَعْرَضْ	يُعْرِضُ	أَعْرَضَ	53
to drown	إغْراق	مُغْرِق	أَغْرِقْ	يُغْرِقُ	أَغْرَقَ	21
to spread corruption	إفْساد	مُفْسِد	أَفْسِدْ	يُفْسِدُ	أَفْسَدَ	36
to be successful	إفْلاح	مُفْلِح	أَفْلِحْ	يُفْلِحُ	أَفْلَحَ	40
to make st grow; to cause to grow	إنْبات	مُنْبِت	أَنْبِتْ	يُنْبِتُ	أَنْبَتَ	16
to warn	إنْذار	مُنْذِرُ	أَنْذِر	يُنْذِرُ	أَنْذَرَ	70
to send down; to reveal	إنْزال	مُنْزِل	أَنْزِلْ	يُنْزِلُ	أَنْزَلَ	190
to produce/create; to make st grow	إنْشاء	مُنْشِئ	أَنْشِئْ	يُنْشِئُ	أَنْشَأَ	22
to favour; to bestow grace	إنْعام	مُنْعِم	أَنْعِم	يُنْعِمُ	أَنْعَمَ	17
to spend	إنْفاق	مُنْفِق	أَنْفِقْ	يُنْفِقُ	أَنْفَقَ	69
to not recognize; to deny	إنْكار	مُنْكِر	أَنْكِر	يُنْكِرُ	أَنْكَرَ	25
to destroy	إهْلاك	مُهْلِك	أَهْلِكْ	يُهْلِكُ	أَهْلَكَ	58

Total words (of this pages): 617   [28]   Percent so far: 78.5

Extra Hamzah before فَعَلَ
(Third person, sing., masc.)

فِعل ثُلاثِي مَزِيد فِيه أَفْعَلَ

to complete	إتْمَام	مُتِمّ	أَتْمِمْ	يُتِمُّ	أَتَمَّ	17
to love	إحْبَاب	مُحِبّ	أَحْبِبْ	يُحِبُّ	أَحَبَّ	64
to make lawful; to cause to dwell	إحْلَال	مُحِلّ	أَحْلِلْ	يُحِلُّ	أَحَلَّ	21
to conceal; to speak secretly	إسْرَار	مُسِرّ	أَسْرِرْ	يُسِرُّ	أَسَرَّ	18
to leave in error; to send astray	إضْلَال	مُضِلّ	أَضْلِلْ	يُضِلُّ	أَضَلَّ	68
to prepare; to make st ready	إعْدَاد	مُعِدّ	أَعْدِدْ	يُعِدُّ	أَعَدَّ	20
to make sb taste	إذَاقَة	مُذِيق	أَذِقْ	يُذِيقُ	أَذَاقَ	22
to intend; to wish	إرَادَة	مُرِيد	أَرِدْ	يُرِيدُ	أَرَادَ	139
to befall; to inflict	إصَابَة	مُصِيب	أَصِبْ	يُصِيبُ	أَصَابَ	65
to obey	إطَاعَة	مُطِيع	أَطِعْ	يُطِيعُ	أَطَاعَ	74
to establish; to set upright	إقَامَة	مُقِيم	أَقِمْ	يُقِيمُ	أَقَامَ	67
to cause someone to die	إمَاتَة	مُمِيت	أَمِتْ	يُمِيتُ	أَمَاتَ	21

Total words (of this pages): 569   [29]   Percent so far: 79.2

Extra Hamzah before نَعَلَ (Third person, sing., masc.						فِعل ثُلاثي مَزِيد فيه أَفعَلَ	
to give life	إحْيَاء	مُحْيِ	أَحْيِ	يُحْيِي	أَحْيَا		53
to conceal	إخْفَاء	مُخْفِ	أَخْفِ	يُخْفِي	أَخْفَى		18
to show	إرَاءَة	مُرِ	أَرِ	يُرِي	أَرَى		44
to enrich	إغْنَاء	مُغْنِ	أَغْنِ	يُغْنِي	أَغْنَى		41
to throw; to cast; to place	إلْقَاء	مُلْقِ	أَلْقِ	يُلْقِي	أَلْقَى		71
to rescue; to save; to deliver	إنْجَاء	مُنْجِ	أَنْجِ	يُنْجِي	أَنْجَى		23
to reveal; to inspire	إيحَاء	مُوحِ	أَوْحِ	يُوحِي	أَوْحَى		72
to fulfil	إيفَاء	مُوفِ	أَوْفِ	يُوفِي	أَوْفَى		18
to believe	إيمَان	مُؤْمِن	آمِن	يُؤْمِنُ	آمَنَ		782
to give	إتْاء	مُؤْتِي	آتِ	يُؤْتِي	آتَى		274
to give trouble; to harm; to annoy16	إيذَاء	مُؤْذِي	آذِ	يُؤْذِي	آذَى		16
passive voice مجهول	→	مُفْعَل		يُفْعَلُ	أَفْعَلَ		

Extra ت and in نَعَل Extra ت and alif in نَعَل		فِعل ثُلاثِي مَزِيد فيه تَفَعَّلَ، تَفَاعَلَ				
	تَفَعَّلْ	مُتَفَعِّل	تَفَعَّل	يَتَفَعَّلُ	تَفَعَّلَ	
to think over; to reflect	تَفَكُّر	مُتَفَكِّر	تَفَكَّر	يَتَفَكَّرُ	تَفَكَّرَ	17
to receive admonition; to remember	تَذَكُّر	مُتَذَكِّر	تَذَكَّر	يَتَذَكَّرُ	تَذَكَّرَ	51
to put one's trust	تَوَكُّل	مُتَوَكِّل	تَوَكَّل	يَتَوَكَّلُ	تَوَكَّلَ	44
to become clear	تَبَيُّن	مُتَبَيِّن	تَبَيَّن	يَتَبَيَّنُ	تَبَيَّنَ	18
to wait and watch for opportunity	تَرَبُّص	مُتَرَبِّص	تَرَبَّص	يَتَرَبَّصُ	تَرَبَّصَ	17
to turn away; to take for friend	تَوَلٍّ	مُتَوَلٍّ	تَوَلَّ	يَتَوَلَّى	تَوَلَّى	79
to make sb die; to receive in full	تَوَفٍّ	مُتَوَفٍّ	تَوَفَّ	يَتَوَفَّى	تَوَفَّى	25
passive voice مجهول	→	مُتَفَعَّل		يُتَفَعَّلُ	تُفُعِّلَ	
	تَفَاعُلْ	مُتَفَاعِل	تَفَاعَلْ	يَتَفَاعَلُ	تَفَاعَلَ	
to be blessed or exalted	تَبَارُك	مُتَبَارِك	تَبَارَكْ	يَتَبَارَكُ	تَبَارَكَ	9
to ask each other	تَسَاؤُل	مُتَسَائِل	تَسَاءَلْ	يَتَسَاءَلُ	تَسَاءَلَ	9

Total words (of this pages): 269   [31]   Percent so far: 81.4

	افْتَعَال	مُفْتَعِل	يَفْتَعِلُ	افْتَعَلَ		Extra alif and ت in نَعَلَ / Extra ا and ن in نَعَلَ فِعل ثُلَاثِي مَزيد فيه افْتَعَلَ، انْفَعَلَ
to differ	اخْتِلَاف	مُخْتَلِف	اخْتَلِفْ	يَخْتَلِفُ	اخْتَلَفَ	52
to follow	اتِّبَاع	مُتَّبِع	اتَّبِعْ	يَتَّبِعُ	اتَّبَعَ	140
to take; to adopt	اتِّخَاذ	مُتَّخِذ	اتَّخِذْ	يَتَّخِذُ	اتَّخَذَ	128
to be on guard; to protect	اتِّقَاء	مُتَّقٍ	اتَّقِ	يَتَّقِي	اتَّقَى	215
to fabricate a lie	افْتِرَاء	مُفْتَرٍ	افْتَرِ	يَفْتَرِي	افْتَرَى	59
to find or to follow the right path	اهْتِدَاء	مُهْتَدٍ	اهْتَدِ	يَهْتَدِي	اهْتَدَى	61
to seek	ابْتِغَاء	مُبْتَغٍ	ابْتَغِ	يَبْتَغِي	ابْتَغَى	48
passive voice مجهول	→	مُفْتَعَل		يُفْتَعَلُ	افْتُعِلَ	
	انْفِعَال	مُنْفَعِل	انْفَعِلْ	يَنْفَعِلُ	انْفَعَلَ	
to turn around; to return	انْقِلَاب	مُنْقَلِب	انْقَلِبْ	يَنْقَلِبُ	انْقَلَبَ	20
to refrain; to end	انْتِهَاء	مُنْتَهٍ	انْتَهِ	يَنْتَهِي	انْتَهَى	16

Total words (of this pages): 739   [32]   Percent so far: 82.33

فِعل ثُلَاثي مَزيد فيه افْعَلَّ، اسْتَفْعَلَ

Extra alif and ل in نَعَلَّ
Extra است **in** نَعَلَ

	افْعِلَال	مُفْعَلٌّ	افْعَلَّ	يَفْعَلُّ	افْعَلَّ	
to become black	اسْوِدَاد	مُسْوَدٌّ	اسْوَدَّ	يَسْوَدُّ	اسْوَدَّ	3
to become white	ابْيِضَاض	مُبْيَضٌّ	ابْيَضَّ	يَبْيَضُّ	ابْيَضَّ	3
passive voice	مُفْعَلٌّ ← مجهول			يُفْعَلُّ	افْعَلَّ	

	اسْتِفْعَال	مُسْتَفْعَلُ	اسْتَفْعِلْ	يَسْتَفْعِلُ	اسْتَفْعَلَ	
to seek ss / to hasten	اسْتِعْجَال	مُسْتَعْجِلٌ	اسْتَعْجِلْ	يَسْتَعْجِلُ	اسْتَعْجَلَ	20
to ask forgiveness	اسْتِغْفَار	مُسْتَغْفِرٌ	اسْتَغْفِرْ	يَسْتَغْفِرُ	اسْتَغْفَرَ	42
to act arrogantly	اسْتِكْبَار	مُسْتَكْبِرٌ	اسْتَكْبِرْ	يَسْتَكْبِرُ	اسْتَكْبَرَ	48
to mock at	اسْتِهْزَاء	مُسْتَهْزِئٌ	اسْتَهْزِئْ	يَسْتَهْزِئُ	اسْتَهْزَأَ	23
to accept; to respond	اسْتِجَابَة	مُسْتَجِيب	اسْتَجِبْ	يَسْتَجِيبُ	اسْتَجَابَ	28
to be able to	اسْتِطَاعَة	مُسْتَطِيع	اسْتَطِعْ	يَسْتَطِيعُ	اسْتَطَاعَ	42
to be straight; to act straight	اسْتِقَامَة	مُسْتَقِيمٌ	اسْتَقِمْ	يَسْتَقِيمُ	اسْتَقَامَ	47
passive voice	مُسْتَفْعَلُ ← مجهول			يُسْتَفْعَلُ	اُسْتُفْعِلَ	

Total words (of this pages): 256   [33]   Percent so far: 82.66

Prepositions that come with the verb and may change the meanings

فِعل + صِلَةُ الْفِعْل

went forth; strove	ضَرَبَ في	came	أَتَى
mentioned	ضَرَبَ لِ	brought	أَتَى بِ
struck upon; overshadowed	ضَرَبَ عَلَى	sought	بَغَى
gave example	ضَرَبَ مَثَلاً	oppressed; was unjust	بَغَى عَلَى
abound	عَفَا	repented	تَابَ، تَابَ إِلَى
forgave	عَفَا عَنْ	accepted the repentance	تَابَ عَلَى
decreed; fulfilled	قَضَى	came, arrived	جَاءَ
judged	قَضَى بَيْنَ	brought	جَاءَ بِ
killed	قَضَى عَلَى	went	ذَهَبَ
put; laid down	وَضَعَ	took away	ذَهَبَ بِ
removed	وَضَعَ عَنْ	went away	ذَهَبَ عَنْ
turned; caused to turn	وَلَّى	was contented	رَضِيَ
turned to	وَلَّى إِلَى	pleased with	رَضِيَ عَنْ
turned away from	وَلَّى عَنْ	stroke	ضَرَبَ

مُذَكَّر Masculine Gender (مَعْرُوف)

	Imperfect Tense	فِعْل مُضَارِع	Past Tense	فِعْل مَاضِي	
ﹹ ه	He does. He will do.	يَفْعَلُ	He did.	فَعَلَ	هُوَ
ﹹ هُمَا	You do/ will do.	يَفْعَلَانِ	They two did.	فَعَلَا	هُمَا
ﹹ هِمْ	They do. They will do.	يَفْعَلُونَ	They all did.	فَعَلُوا	هُمْ
ـكَ	You do. You will do.	تَفْعَلُ	You did.	فَعَلْتَ	أَنْتَ
ـكُمَا	You do/will do.	تَفْعَلَانِ	You two did.	فَعَلْتُمَا	أَنْتُمَا
ـكُمْ	You all do. You all will do.	تَفْعَلُونَ	You all did.	فَعَلْتُمْ	أَنْتُمْ
ـي ني	I do. I will do.	أَفْعَلُ	I did.	فَعَلْتُ	أَنَا
ـنَا	We do. We will do.	نَفْعَلُ	We did.	فَعَلْنَا	نَحْنُ

Masculine Gender مُذَكَّر

Negative نهي		Imperative أمر		
Don't do!	لَا تَفْعَلْ	Do!	افْعَلْ	Singular
Don't (you two) do!	لَا تَفْعَلَا	Do (you two)!	افْعَلَا	Dual
Don't (you all) do!	لَا تَفْعَلُوا	Do (you all)!	افْعَلُوا	Plural

				مَجْهُول
(it) is being done.	يُفْعَلُ	(it) is done.	فُعِلَ	Passive voice

Passive participle	اسم مفعول	Active participle	اسم فاعل	
The one who is affected.	مَفْعُول	Doer.	فَاعِل	Singular
	مَفْعُولَان، مَفْعُولَيْن		فَاعِلَان، فَاعِلَيْن	Dual
	مَفْعُولُون، مَفْعُولِين		فَاعِلُون، فَاعِلِين	Plural

		مصدر
action; act of doing	فِعْل …	Noun of action

(مَعْرُوف) Feminine Gender مُؤَنَّث

	Imperfect Tense	فِعْل مُضَارِع	Past Tense	فِعْل مَاضِي	
ـُهَا	She does. She will do.	تَفْعَلُ	She did.	فَعَلَتْ	هِيَ
ـُهُمَا	You do/will do.	تَفْعَلَانِ	They two did.	فَعَلَتَا	هُمَا
ـُهُنَّ	They do. They will do.	يَفْعَلْنَ	They all did.	فَعَلْنَ	هُنَّ
ـكَ	You do. You will do.	تَفْعَلِينَ	You did.	فَعَلْتَ	أَنْتِ
ـكُمَا	You do/will do.	تَفْعَلَانِ	You two did.	فَعَلْتُمَا	أَنْتُمَا
ـكُنَّ	You all do. You all will do.	تَفْعَلْنَ	You all did.	فَعَلْتُنَّ	أَنْتُنَّ
ـي ـنِي	I do. I will do.	أَفْعَلُ	I did.	فَعَلْتُ	أَنَا
ـنَا	We do. We will do.	نَفْعَلُ	We did.	فَعَلْنَا	نَحْنُ

Feminine Gender مُؤَنَّث

Negative نهي		Imperative أمر		
Don't do!	لَا تَفْعَلِي	Do!	اِفْعَلِي	Singular
Don't (you two) do!	لَا تَفْعَلَا	Do (you two)!	اِفْعَلَا	Dual
Don't (you all) do!	لَا تَفْعَلْنَ	Do (you all)!	اِفْعَلْنَ	Plural

(it) is being done.	تُفْعَلُ	(it) is done.	فُعِلَتْ	مَجْهُول Passive voice

Passive participle	اسم مفعول	Active participle	اسم فاعل	
The one who is affected.	مَفْعُولَة	Doer.	فَاعِلَة	Singular
	مَفْعُولَان، مَفْعُولَيْن		فَاعِلَتَان، فَاعِلَتَيْن	Dual
	مَفْعُولُون، مَفْعُولِين		فَاعِلَات	Plural

action; act of doing	... فِعْل	مصدر Noun of action

Made in the USA
Las Vegas, NV
03 May 2024

89478913R00031